The Universal Language of Love

Hassen G. Alli
The Universal Language of Love

Published by Spines
ISBN: 978-965-578-935-5

To my Mother Lolita,
The way you loved me has made me the man and the lover I am
today. All the endeavors I continue to pursue in this life are an
attempt to honor your memory & to continue to make you proud.

To my Readers,
Thank you for giving my words a chance to resonate and be heard
in your world. I hope you are inspired, encouraged, and challenged
to love even harder & live life vividly; continuing to embrace
moments of love along the way.

To those I've loved,
Thanks for the lessons and enlightenment gained through our
interactions & time spent in love. Loving you has allowed me to see,
share, & spread my love more genuinely & for that I am thankful.

Table of Contents

The Universal Language of Love

LOVE'S CYCLE DEPICTED THROUGH A COLLECTION OF 51 POEMS

HASSEN G. ALLI

Untitled

I'm not too good with words
So let me write this down
I'm kind of, sort of, getting used to having you around
I know it may sound funny
Or even out of line
I'm feeling who & what you are
And I want to make you mine
Friends? Or maybe more, that's totally up to you
You're a good friend & person
No matter what you choose to do
I just need to know soon
Fill me in before it's too late
I'm rushing you to do this
Because feelings aren't that easy to erase

Untitled

Less than Zero
A negative One
A day without sunshine
A child without fun
》This is me without you
A song without words
An ocean without waves
A sky without birds
A week without days
》This is me without you
A life with no meaning
A pocket with no money
A night's rest without dreaming
A bee's hive with no honey
》This is me without you
A pantry with no food
A birthday without cake
A world without good
Having a figure with no shape
》 This is me without you
》》 I am nothing....

Untitled

I'm going out of my mind
Thinking about you all of the time
You've found someone else
And I feel all by myself
I should be over you
But somehow I'm not
Love's lesson is over
But I haven't been taught
Sitting & waiting & contemplating why
When I should just face it and tell you goodbye
Love has been lost & will never be found
What hurts me the most is that you're still around
Although you're still near me
And the next will have their turn
I've Ushered in new thinking
And realized I'm gonna have to Let It Burn

Untitled

I like the way you make me feel
The simple way you keep it real
The way you know just what to say
Like we could talk all damn day
I can't say that I've known you for that very long
But I can say that my feelings are becoming very strong
It's almost like you're perfect, the one I've been looking for
Like my heart has been closed all this time
And you just opened the door
Like symphonies in paradise, you make me feel at ease
Like a cool winter morning, or a warm summer breeze
Just a touch from you seems to satisfy my needs
Needs that have been contained
Needs in which you freed
Never before now have I ever felt like this
How I want to be near you & how I miss your kiss
Your soft lips, your eyes, your hands I miss too
But what I miss most is just being with you
It's truly amazing how you affect me
You turn me on; mind, soul, & body
It's hard to imagine that I'll ever be
In love with someone like I am with thee

Untitled

You threw me for a loop & now you got me thinking twice
Knowing how & what you feel right now would be real nice
But I don't & that's bugging me
As I find myself struggling
To gather my thoughts, as I sort out my doubts
My mind & body tired of trying to figure you out
Was it something that I did or maybe said? Is it me?
Is it something you haven't told me that you should have in the
beginning?
All these thoughts in my head, racing ever so constantly
Am I trippin'? Maybe
But it's just this one thing that's got me stuck on you
But I ain't mad, I still love you
No matter what baby I do, I swear that this is true
But no one likes to look stupid & that's kind of how I feel
Is there something going on?
Let your baby know the deal
But I hope that it's just nothing
Soon this will all be funny
And we'll still be together
....like bees & honey
I hope that made you laugh because I love to see you smile
Although I haven't in a while, you still drive me wild
Bottom line all I'm asking is for more of your time
With 24 hours in a day, can at least 1 be mine?
This is all a big side effect of me missing you
I don't feel at all sick, but I think I caught the "U"
Because it's "U" that I think about
It's "U" that's got me
It's "U" that I dream about
With "U's" where I wanna be
It's "U" that I love... I Love "U"

Untitled

What you always want
Is not what you always get
Sometimes in life you just have to deal with it
Yearning for the best & getting something much less
Aiming for the top, yet always being stopped
In a state of depression is where you'll soon find yourself
In this state of pure need, you can't even be helped
With no one to talk to, no one who knows how you feel
No difference exists between what's fake & what's real
Because it's all just the same; one big game
And in your body & brain
You're becoming physically insane
With less ups than downs
No smiles & all frowns
It feels like chaos and disaster are happening all around
But it's not the end of the world
Just keep trying & don't you quit
Because there's somethings that you'll want
And for now you cannot get

Untitled

Doing what you have to do & not even trying
Struggling to live & inside you're just dying
Emotionally hurt, physically crying
Your life is on hold & time is just winding
You say something today & forget it tomorrow
With no intentions to payback
You constantly borrow
You continue to live & do things the old way
And all the while you don't realize you're shortening your days
Working paycheck to paycheck with no break in between
The world is against you, or so it seems
Thanks to those like Dr. Martin Luther King
Because of these people I now have a dream
To make this a better world starting with myself
To do away with old habits
And help those who need to be helped
To make me a better person & make sure that whatever I do
If not onto others, to myself always be true

Untitled

Is it the smell or is it the feel
That reassures me that this is real
Not some artificial fragrance
But the most authentic sensation
Is something that comes over me
Whenever you are holding me; or right here next to me
The place you fit so perfectly
A place I thought I'd never be
Hand in hand, two human beings
Exploring & open to eL Oh Vee Ee
With a taste of life's finer things
Like a simple mutual complicity
You see, it's been about.... An eternity
Since I thought of & believed in these feelings
Of sharing tender moments & creating memories
Doing all the things that people often seem –
To forget are important & life's true reasoning;
Loving, Caring, Providing for
Taking you out & opening doors
Protect you, Love you, Give you more
Show you what you've been waiting for
Show you the point & both curves of my heart
The way I feel now, I've felt straight from the start
The lower part of your back is pure royalty
The spot on your neck, behind your ear makes me weak
This is starting to feel like the epitome
Of what our love life could really be...
Just you & me

Untitled

I'm trapped in this place
In a house by my spouse
Like a mouse in a dark hole
And the only glimpse of light you stole
Like a thief in the night
At a time not so right
When everything already is not so bright
And here you come to steal my light
Good thing I keep batteries
In case of bad things happening
Like people coming after me
And stealing my light is their strategy
But I say this not too sadly;
Not this time! It's a tragedy!
Nope, it's quite miraculous
That I can rise & overcome this
That I can experience, learn, & understand
That I came into this equipped with a back-up plan
That there you go, but here I stand
A stronger, wiser, better man
More than ever was, more than you can ever be
You stole my light, but I still can see

Happy Day

As beautiful as a rose
As delicate as a feather
The right to love you
Should be treasured forever
We haven't been together for long
But I think it's time I say
You are Wonderful
You are Amazing
Happy (Valentine's Day)
Happy (Anniversary)
Happy (Birthday)

Homecoming Night

Tonight's a special night
The stars are shining ever so bright
And everything about you is looking oh so right
Your hair, your dress from head to toe
The way you look tonight is guaranteed to steal the show
Your face is so gorgeous
Your body is so fine
I'm honored to say that for tonight, you're all mine
Well it's almost that time when the night will soon begin
As we walk through those doors together hand in hand
We'll dance the night away & have the time of our lives
You & me here together on this Homecoming Night

Valentine's

A few words for my Valentine
Will you be mine?
Because you [Insert Name] are one of a kind
You've blown my mind
You're so damn fine
I find myself thinking of you all of the time
I respect the fact that you stay on your grind
Smart, Strong, & Focused
Today a rare find
Beautiful, Soft, & Unique
All are other signs
That on this day of Valentine's
We're together you & I
To share this day with [Insert Name], truly precious time
And you my precious, are one of a kind.

Perfection

You're so f****** perfect, & it's way more than your looks
Tell everybody, put this in the books!

Oh, you're so perfect, You made my heart stop
All the things that make you up from the bottom to the top

This is why you are perfect & everyone can see
That big thing that you carry...your crown, you're a king

Why are you so perfect? It's really not fair
Seeing you pass, why not stop and stare?

You are so damn perfect & I want you to know
So I'm using my actions & I want them to show

[Insert Name] you are perfect but this you already knew
Because you are perfect & perfect is you.

All About You

This is all about YOU
So I'll start with the Y
Why YOU are so special & how YOU caught my eye
How YOU are simply a different kind of guy
I've said it before, YOU are one of a kind
YOU're just like a star up in the sky
YOU are forever
YOU are always on my mind
YOU are the reason why time flies
YOU could really be the love of my life
Why oh why are YOU so YOU
YOU are perfect
Because YOU are YOU

The 1

A year since the beginning
A year it has been
1 year ago today is when I met my best friend
The 1 who has been there through BIG ups & downs
The 1 who has gone but is still somehow around
The 1 who has left but always seems to come back
The 1 who gets me off but yet keeps me on track
The 1 I'm proud of, that I love, whom I adore
The 1 I call my [Insert term of endearment] now & forever more
So cheers to the years & to all of the above
This is for us, for life, for ever, & for love

Spirit of Love

In the beginning there's this feeling
That you really can't describe
A feeling that consumes you
And burns within you deep inside
A feeling you can't hold back
And that you cannot even hide
This feeling becomes who you are
And starts to take over your life
A feeling for someone, for something, somehow
A feeling that when you're losing, you won't throw in the towel
This feeling is like a spirit
Like the breath in which you breathe
A spirit that will keep you still
No matter how badly you want to leave

100%

You may think that I'm playing
But really what I'm saying
Is that I kind of like the way that you got me behaving
Constantly in my heart
And forever on my mind
Thinking about my baby 99% of the time
And the other 1% I'm thinking about us
And how strong we've become
And how you I can trust
I really like this feeling of love and belonging
The feeling I get from my sweetie, my darling
It's a fresh feeling
Something special, something new
A feeling that I feel only when I'm with you

Where I Wanna Be

A small place in your heart
Would be fine by me
A brief description of where I wanna be
In the most beautiful paradise, living in luxury
Behind guarded doors, just you & me
In an unforeseen place, full of mystery
A quaint, quiet atmosphere
Possessing simple things
Total chaos can surround us
But in the middle it's you and me
Just like the eye of a storm;
Calm as can be
In a place filled with nothing
Us there would mean everything
In a place full of limits, we'd be infinity
Where our only company is time & gravity
And everything else is just mere fantasy
Only with myself & you
And obviously you & me
That is a place
Where I wanna be

Love You Always

If I can't have you no one can
I'll never stop loving you
That's the way I am
Seeing you with someone else, I just couldn't stand
Seeing you in the arms of another man?
I'll never accept this, it's just too much to bear
Although you might not think so, I still do really care
And even though I know that this situation is unfair
I hope that you'll realize that our love was rare
For this one reason you should give us another chance
Warm memories that I have keep my heart in this trance
...of loving you and only you & I swear that this is true;
No one can ever love you the way that I do
No one could ever do for you the things that I could
No one would ever treat you the way that I would
These are just a couple of words, simply just to say
That I love you now & forever
And I'll love you always

One of a Kind

One of a kind
Kind of the One
In a sky full of stars
You are a Sun
When I miss you, I need you
When I see you, I feel you
Not with you, Think of you
Sleeping, Dream of you

To be near you, safe
To hold you, tight
To hear you, comforting
To be yours feels right
The sight of you, breath taking
Like magic in the making
When you speak, you're commanding
Your words are enchanting
My passions you ignite
My heart you excite
Like always on my mind
You are One of a kind

-
-
-
-
-
-
-
-
-

The feeling you give is irreplaceable
If not from you then unattainable
My heart & thoughts you fill
You're genuine, You're real
You're special, You're a king
You're a man of many things
You're beautiful & unique
You're everything in between

Your smile is love
And your eyes are wonder
You are truly like no other
You alter my mind
You've changed how I feel
It seems with you
My destiny's fulfilled
One day I hope to call you all mine
And that we will stand the test of time...
Hand in Hand, Side by Side
Two of us, One of a kind

In 10 Days

It's only been 10 days
And in 10 different ways
I feel my outlook on love has drastically changed
Moving fast & jumping in
All cards on the table, hoping to win
Losing myself in the light brown of your eyes
Then finding myself not wanting to leave your side
It's an overwhelming feeling that has come over me
Could this be love? ...Real love? ....Already?
Is this just you, or could it just be me?
Or is this all just one big dream?
If so I'll stay asleep for as long as I can
Not wanting to wake up & lose grip of your hand
Or lose sight of the thought of your height when you stand
Or for you to disappear from my real life; this dream man
When you touch me it feels real
When we kiss & when we lay
When we connect intimately, it feels real in other ways
I've been thinking of words to simply say,
That basically I Love You at the end of the day
Too soon you may say & I'm still not ashamed
Day two I felt this way, but I waited eight more days to say
That this is how I feel & I feel like this is real
So here's to letting you in on this here day 10

Dear You,

I don't know why I be feeling like this. I guess I just love you. I don't see how after all the drama I put no one before you. When times get hard you're never there, and when I hurt inside it seems as if you don't even care. Am I the stupid one for loving you still? Or is love the stupid one for knowing that I will? Days without a word from you; weeks even months. Those nights I just lay in bed, longing for your touch. I extinguish this fire within me that burns so hot for you, & yet you re-kindle it with the simple things you do. I forget you and somehow you remember me. I'm beginning to think that there must be a conspiracy. When we talk, we click so well it's almost like you're kin to me. I'm so blessed to have known such a wonderful human being. But yet I still wonder if you're even into me. I'm 1 & 2, and I want for you to be that number 3. In some ways it's like without you I feel so incomplete. GOD damn you don't know how much I want you right here next to me. To hold you and to love you so that our love can truly grow. I need no money, cars, or jewels for my love will truly show; How much I want you, and want for you to want me. I need to know if you love me, write me back ASAP.

Sincerely,
Me.

Just Two Words

You me
To gether
In love
Just 'cuz
Make love
For fun
Me you
Become one
One love
You I
All alone
Hearts tied
We love
We die
In heaven
We fly
I You
Us two

-
-
-
-
-
-
-
-
-
-

Never part
Purple hearts
We share
Beat strong
Live long
Love song
Sweet dreams
You mean
The world
To me
Every thing
Just us
Two words
Just two
All Trust
Love you
I do
Any thing
For you

Love You More

I don't think it's possible to love as hard as I do
After heartbreak, nonsense, & bullshit
I somehow still miss you
You've caused this pain
These feelings that I feel
Not knowing the difference between what's fake & what's real
I can't even imagine what life would be like
Doing this thing without you right by my side
I love you through the pain, through the tears, through the rain
When I probably shouldn't stay
Beside you I'll remain
My view of you is crazy, it's like you can do no wrong
You break me down, then build me up;
This is clearly your love song
When will you realize, with me, everything you got
Loyalty, love, & laughter
But there it doesn't stop
I cherish you, appreciate you, I literally kiss your feet
I honor & obey you, like you really are my King
You are my favorite person
My favorite human being
I love you like mucho
Probably more than you love me
And for that I'll always feel stupid
Because that's a silly place to be,
To love someone else more than I love me

T-O-G-E-T-H-E-R

I just want to be with you
Is that too much to ask ?
Us together would be perfect
I know we'd make it last
Just the thought of you & I is satisfying for me
I find myself content in your carefree company
Every minute that I'm with you seems to brighten up my day
And your smile would be enough to ease any pain away
It's hard to express myself or even let you know how I feel
I give you hints & little clues but I know you know the deal
I just want a chance to show you what life would be like
To spoil you
To love you
To have you in my life
But maybe you are right
Maybe it's best that we remain friends
The physical aspect of my love may stop but mentally it won't end
I've felt this way for some time now though I haven't let it show
Getting this stuff off my chest will enable me to grow
I really want us to be together but is that even meant to be ?
I've waited this long so far and I'm still willing to wait & see

Kiss

A way of life
A reason to live
When you find that person you just want to give
Your heart & soul
Your body & mind
You think of this person all of the time
You really truly can't explain how you feel
And all you can say is you know it's for real
All day and all night, when you're awake & when you're asleep
You anticipate the moment when your lips will again meet
Their beautiful body & smooth brown skin
Eyes so deep they simply have no end
The way they walk, the air they breathe
You hate the moment when they have to leave
You love being around them
Just their presence turns you on
Though you're not together now
You've wanted them for so long
Simply the sound of their voice seems to make your day
And you wish you could find the words to just say;
I care so much for you & you should know this
I can't wait for the next time that you & I Kiss

Nice and Slow

I softly kiss your neck & gently caress your face
Preparing your body for what's about to take place
Our temperatures are rising
I feel your body heat
I love the way your body feels right on top of me
Back & forth
Up & down
As we begin to move
Trying to keep it steady
Not messing up the groove
You feel my tongue in places you have never felt before
I try to stop & slow it down but you tell me you want more
I feel your nails across my back
You grip me tighter as I speed up
It feels so good you & me together slowly making sweet love
I whisper softly in your ear to ask if you're alright
My body craves your body's touch
Making love all night

Down

It's a different position don't get me wrong
I guess I just love the scent of your thong
I kiss your lips tenderly but yours don't kiss back
Because the lips I'm kissing aren't supposed to kiss back
I'm caressing your body in a way different from the rest
Making love if you will, but not quite having sex
Your legs on my shoulders, my chin to your waist
My appetite is calling for your body's special taste
Ass up, heads down I'm the best around
Especially when it comes to going down town
It makes me happy to know that you're enjoying me
As I open up your candy store & begin to eat your sweets
On Monday
It's your Twizzler that I'm always dreaming about
On Tuesday
It's the Skittles you be popping in my mouth
On Wednesday
It's your Snickers that I simply just adore
On Thursday
It's your cookie that keeps me coming back for more
On Friday through Sunday
Most dudes would give it a rest
But on the weekends baby
Is when I do it best
Whether you like it rough & tough or real cool & smooth
I've got a different lick to satisfy your every mood
My Tornado Tongue & my Lickety Split
My moves will make you forget all about dick
And don't ever worry about me running out
Because there's always a little left for me down south

No Strings Attached

A kiss here & there
A call every now & then
A simple conversation to find out how you've been
We decide to meet up at that same special place
I get off at six, so I'll meet you there around eight
We meet, we greet, we grab a bite to eat
I pay, we leave, & now it's time for that treat
We find a cozy place not too near but not too far
And make that transition to the back of the car
I take off your clothes & you take off mine
I don't recall from last time your body being this fine
We rub & touch as we do what we do
And before we both know it, we're already through
This time we dress ourselves & now it's time to leave
The ride back is so silent
I can actually hear you breathe
As I drop you off I feel like my heart is being snatched
And I don't know why
Because we both know there's no strings attached

Tragic Sex

So deep inside & not feeling a thing
Sex without feelings is a tragedy

Being connected & coming together as one
Only to leave, then feel all alone

Taking my words, not saying them back
A race to the finish, then done just like that

Only for a moment, then on to the next
To sum it up nicely, meaningless sex

Or fucking forever, with no sign of a ring
Sex without feelings is a tragedy

When I share me, I'm letting you in
Risking it all, a purposeful sin

You leave me with nothing, left searching again
For something long lasting; a companion, a friend

Holding this in, keeping it tight
Something so wrong that feels so right

Needing much more, it's easy to see
Sex without feelings is a tragedy

My True Feelings

When I first met you everything was real cool
I'd see you all the time
We'd hang out after school
But things began to change
I really don't know why
I don't want to just give up
I'd rather stay & try
To work things out and hold on to what's between you & me
I'm starting to think this relationship was never meant to be
We barely get to talk & now I hardly see you at all
I can't even remember the last time that you called
It's hard enough to let go of something that I love so much
I miss the simple things like your kiss, hug, & touch
I try to block out what others say because I know it's just mess
The current state of this relationship is causing me so much stress
I wish you'd take the time to tell me how you feel
I don't ask much of you but just to keep it real
I wish things would go back to the way they used to be
When I was in love with you & you were in love with me

Will We

Will we last
Will we be
Will I choose you
Will you choose me
Will this make us better
Will this be forever
Will we make it through
Will we say I do
Will you miss the things of the past
Will we put in the work to make us last
Will I do things I've done before
Will we give love a chance once more
Will we continue to experience new things
Will you realize what all this means
Will you say Yes & take this ring
Will you & me officially become we

Secret Love

A secret love affair with you is what I'd love to have
Where no one knows what's going on except you & me
Your secret is mine and mine is yours & baby you know I won't tell

We can do all the things that "open" lovers do
But only behind "closed" doors
We can hold hands & hold bodies as long as no one knows
For your secrets are mine and mine are yours & baby you know I
won't tell

Because loving you so secretly is what I've always wanted to do
Secretly seeing each other & whispering that I love you
You know my secret is yours and yours are mine & baby I won't tell

Meeting up at places, posing as best friends, really hiding the truth
When deep down we know what we're holding back within us
You know your secret's mine and my secret's yours, & baby I
won't tell

Drifting off to sleep the last thing that crosses my mind is you
Sometimes I pray to GOD to be blessed with a dream of you...
You, me, & GOD are the only ones who know
And for now that's as far as it will ever go
Because your secret is mine and mine is yours & baby you know I
won't tell

My Fault

A simple memory of a loved one that slowly fades away
Something you loved so dearly suddenly disappeared one day
You sit and think it over & all you have left to say
Is that you're the sole reason why things are this way
I wish I could turn back the mighty hands of time
I put no blame on you
For the fault is all mine
You sentenced me to life, & yes I did the crime
But I don't see why you can't let the past stay behind
I urge you to move forward
Athough I stay stuck on you
I'm constantly reminded by everything that I do
When I'm alone, or at work; at home or in my car
I'm constantly reminded of how beautiful you are
The only one I truly loved
My soulmate by far
In a crowd of a million, you're that one shining star
So I don't see why you keep your love locked up in a vault
When I'm telling you I realize & know it was my fault

Still N Love

I know that I still love you
But do you still love me?
I've been counting the days since you've been gone; 343
Almost a year has passed & still I think of thee
Still curious & wondering
Do you still think of me?
Do you think of all our time together?
The good times and the bad?
The times I made you happy?
The times I made you mad?
The times we said we'd be together until the end of time?
The times we disagreed and I took back things of mine?
I know I did things wrong that I simply can't take back
But never did I mean for us to end up where we're at;
Apart from one another, you not next to me
Not only physically apart, but also mentally
So do you still think of me?
Because of you I still do
And this is how I know that I still love you

In Details

Since it's details you like, let me go into depth
About what I think & how I feel about you step by step
I think of your face, I think of your smile
I think about if one day I'll call you all mine
I think of your voice & the way that you sound
I even think of how you think
And how your every word drives me wild
I think of you every day of the week
I'm thinking of you when I'm awake
I'm thinking of you when I'm asleep
I like what I know & what I don't know even better
It's the absence of you here that brings us closer together
If time was to teach, I'd say we hadn't learned much
And life lessons from the past won't allow me to rush
However with you I feel safe, it feels good
I know that I'll treat you better than anyone could
At this steady pace, I knew it wouldn't be long
Before we become one with a love so strong
And before love has been learned & together we move on
...Further in details, into another chapter

Searching through love's book for our happily ever after
Circling the things right, & crossing out the wrongs
Picking out every detail, like your favorite songs;
Killing me softly is what you do to me
And without you girl, My Life is Incomplete
These Love Games you play keep me Dangerously in Love
Between Crazy, Sexy, & Cool, you're all of the above
My baby, My Sweet Lady, it's just like Déjà vu,
Cuz' tonight baby, I Wanna Get Freaky with You!
The way you talk when I do
The way you crack a smile
And the way I feel you feel for me really drives me wild
Damn near the perfect person; all around, in & out
You are my favorite person, definitely no doubt
Although you're now there & I am here
The short distance between us will not persevere
For I would travel this world in hopes of finding the same you
And do whatever, whenever to ensure that I do
Let the world be our classroom, & the two things we'd discuss
Would be the ins and outs of our Love & Trust

Dear You 2,

I still haven't heard from you. I don't know what's the deal with that. I told you we needed to talk and yet you haven't wrote me back. I've been at home all alone, just waiting to hear back from you. You've been out with your friends doing whatever the hell it is that you do. I told you how I felt, but I guess you just don't get it. The first letter I wrote meant nothing, although I put my whole heart in it. Oh yeah, remember that shit I said before about 1, 2, & 3? Since I've gotten no response from you, disregard the whole damn thing. You see I'm trying to keep my cool with you, though you make it difficult for me. I'm writing you this letter, but damn, can you even see? My heart still longs for you, you're the one I want to be with. You're like a drug that's ruining my life & yet I still can't quit. With each breath that I take and every word that I write, I envision us together again & everything's alright. Just so that you know, to my heart you still have the key, but do me this one favor please... write me back ASAP.

Sincerely,
Me.

Bitter / Sweet

It all comes down to a degree of separation
A level we have reached due to my inattentive behavior
Though it hurts to think that you and I will split
I trust in your word that it's best like this
And I know that's it's best for us to be at our best
Giving our friendship a test, by putting our relationship to a rest
An unconditional love, that's how it should be
But in the condition I'm in now
Only your love can cure me
Because I feel as if without you I'll just die
But I'll pull myself together & I'll continually try
To perfect myself for the perfect guy
Anticipating us reuniting as the days go by
My love for you is everlasting
And that should go without asking
My feelings are so deep
They'd out flood the deepest sea
Feelings that exceed the simple touch of a hand
Just as you exceed my expectations of a man
Though I may cry myself to sleep,
Or sit in my bed and weep
I'll still dream of you & me
And how one day you will see;
How I've changed for you
How little we've been through
And all the things I now do
Are because I really love you...

Played Out

Love is not a game
Although I feel I'm being played
Should I leave or should I stay?
Should I really feel this way?
How much am I really worth to you?
Why don't you love me like you suppose to?
These are the things I think about
That are really starting to drain me out
I'd love to know you love me
This is something that I need
I'd love to know you love me
Do you even know what that means?
You're just not getting it
There must be something in between
Wish I could wake up & scream
And all this would just be a dream
But it's not you're really here
And I still do really care
But are you even aware?
Of my pain and despair?
If you're playing me please stop
For my heart has already dropped
As far as it will go
I just can't take it anymore
....I'm gone

Shady Lover

Feeling a way that I shouldn't
Saying things that I wouldn't
Being kind of shady is a simple way to put it
Acting in a way that's strictly forbidden
Doing little shit & keeping it hidden
Two wrongs don't make it right
I see how this is true
But when you have one wrong & one right
Then what are you to do?
Do you go with your gut feeling
Or sit and contemplate?
This situation is a two-way street;
One is love & one is hate
Captured in a love triangle you can't even think straight
No matter how hard you try, you simply just can't
Do you satisfy yourself, your friend, or your love?
Or do you try to find a way to do all of the above?
Do you continue on with your sneaky ways?
Or confess to your friend for future brighter days?
Should you lie to your lover & tell them it's through?
Knowing damn well that's not what you really want to do?
Are you actually being shady,
Or simply just behaving
The way a normal person would, if they only understood
How you really felt, how you just can't help yourself
A shady lover in much need of help

Is It Worth It?

Is it worth it sometime or is it just a mistake
Is it worth it sometimes all the time that it takes
Is it worth it with all the pain that you have to endure
Is it worth it to be rich now & to still end up poor
Is it worth it to now love but to never love again
Was it worth all that going through to end up just as friends
Is it worth all the talking if you're not getting anywhere
Is it worth giving your all if no one even cares
Is it worth all the sacrifices, the worries, & the strife
Is it worth it to have it now
But to owe someone for the rest of your life
Is it worth it to be beautiful & invisible too
Is beauty so beautiful if no one can really see you
Is it worth lowering your standards to be like everyone else
Is it worth fitting in if you can't just be yourself
Is it worth having the world with no one to share it with
Is it worth looking both ways if you're still bound to get hit
Is it worth crying now if you'll just look back & laugh
Was it worth crying in the first place for something you never had
So, is it worth it in the end
When you're done, when you're through
Is it worth it is a question left up to only you

Hate POEM

You can't stand this certain person
Just their name makes you sick
You hate this dumbass, motherfuckin', evil, lying bitch
They constantly smile in your face & do shit behind your back
If you find out some more lies
Somebody's getting slapped
Just be real, suck it up, & tell me to my face
If you'd like I'd even give you the time, date, & place
But you'll never do that
You're just too damn afraid
If you were a roach, I'd have yo' ass screaming RAID!
Because that's what I want to do; exterminate you & be through
But this is my life & I can't let your stupidity affect the things I do
You whisper lies in my ears
Lies you use to hide your fears
You think I'm still shedding tears?
GTFUOH
Your words now mean nothing
Mere air that you breathe
A couple more lessons & your ass just might see
That lies and mess amount to nothing & cheating is a disease
And since this is your diagnosis
You won't find the cure with me
Try following this one rule:
Tell the truth & speak only what you know
When lies invite you over, simply just don't fucking go
So if this has you thinking about who, what, & why
Just think a little harder about the person I described

Why Can't I Ever Reach You?

Why can't I ever reach you?
When I call you're never there
When I stop by to say I love you
I'm greeted by only air
Why can't I ever reach you?
Is a question that lies in me
When you should be home & on the phone
You're out there in the streets
Why can't I ever reach you?
It's something I'd like to know
Because it's best we keep in touch
If we want this relationship to grow
Now I start to reach you
I see you've had a change of heart
But is this the beginning of the end
Or a quick finish to a start?
Now I start to reach you
When I call you actually pick up

And when I come to meet you
You're there to greet me with a hug
Now I start to reach you
And it really does feel good
But to get to this point I had to wait
Just a bit longer than I should
Now you can never reach me
And you're like, What's the deal with that?
It's funny now I got you thinking
Where's this nigah at?
Now you can never reach me
You're clearly upset & this I see
But you had your fun, your time is up
And now it's all about me
Now you can never reach me
Turns out you're not that strong
It's just so sad it took you this long
To see that I've moved on

Meant To Be

I get it now
We came into this world alone
Because that's the way we're Meant To Be
No one to talk to on the phone
No one to love you endlessly
No one to share good company
No one to just be with carefree
No one to live with happily
No one anymore seems Meant To Be
Because there's always something, when it's nothing
And when there's nothing, it's still something
Most of the time it really is nothing
And we still make it out to be something
And then pop! There goes my balloon of reality
As my world starts dripping down all around me
And everything now becomes plain to see
That you & I aren't Meant To Be
You were never really real with me
Funny how this always ends up happening
Only now that you're gone can I truly see
That's just the way things are Meant To Be...Alone

New Beginnings

Aw here we go, as my heart begins to open up
And you remind me of those feelings of a budding new love
My head begins to fill with simple thoughts of you
My heart begins to fill because of the simple things you do
Trying things different so not to jeopardize
Any future opportunities to look deep into your eyes
Conveying subtly that I want you to be close
Showing you I'm interested without doing the most
Taking it slow so that we may grow
But only in the direction that GOD says so
Loco, Fou, Verrückt; Are foreign ways to say
How you've had me feeling these past couple of days
We text like crazy; I look forward to it
I can't wait till we start & I never want to quit
My turn, your turn, your turn, mine
I be having too much to text half the damn time
But I have a lot to say
You make me feel a lot of ways
Like sunshine does to rain
You really brighten up my day
Like the opposite of pain
You bring joy my way
I know it sounds cliché, but you make me feel so gay
I care about what you think, what you want, how you feel
I never want to let you down
I always want to keep it real
Showing you the real me is only what you deserve
Raising THE standard & setting THE curve
Just take my hand & in return give me yours
We'll move forward together
Opening up new doors

Scared of Love

I'm scared of us changing & us rearranging
These feelings we feel
For something even more real
A commitment of sorts
Exclusive of course
Never been here before
Wanting so much more
At least not like this
Longing for your kiss
Yearning for your touch
How I miss you so much
This feeling that's come over me
Is taking whole control of me
Seeing things I never see
Being treated so lovingly
Caught up in your company
You make me feel so bubbly
Thoughts of you; Just comforting

-
-
-
-
-
-
-
-
-

Next to you is where I want to be
In your arms & you under me
Chest to chest when you're holding me
You're my King, my majesty
So let me ask you this one thing
Does it have to be that frightening?
Just the thought of you & me?
Together forever, happily
Living life lavishly?
I'm scared but I am ready
As ready as I'll ever be
To give you all of me
To fall with you hopelessly
So join me on this journey
A marathon to eternity
I've got you & you got me
TRUE love isn't that scary...

Done in the Dark

What's done in the dark will always come to the light
Sometimes from what you feel
Sometimes from insight
Intuition or spiritually;
What's meant for you, you WILL eventually see
When things don't seem right & everything's a mystery
And you find yourself always confused as can be
Stressing out & thinking constantly
Racking your brain over the same stupid things
Silly thoughts in your head & you can't get them out
You pray & deflect but they still come about
Sometimes when you're looking
More often when you're not
Knowing things with no proof is a pretty tough spot
Making decisions with half truths never turns out right
It only causes regrets, urges for revenge, & spite
And these things only negatively impact your life
All the while people act like everything's alright
The main take away from this is always focus on the good
And trust that things always happen just as they should
For better or for worse
No matter how hard the fight
What's done in the dark will always come to the light

In Due Time

You piss on me, you shit on me
You fuck me up mentally
Thought this could be
Nope this ain't for me
Because I know my worth
More than rocks & dirt
Putting me next to empty bottoms really hurts
Since I hold you so high like a GOD.....wait that's it!
You eclipse my whole world & I can't see shit!
I thought you were perfect & us a good fit
And that in due time we could work on it
Like taking the time to find the ins & outs
And seeing what you're really all about
Like what makes you laugh?
What makes you, you?
What makes you do the dumbass shit that you do?
What makes you smile?
How can I make you mine?
How are you walking around here so precious & so fine?
But in due time we'll see
That our little situation can't be
Different level shit, you're you & I'm me
Nothing better, nothing bad
Just not the Ss Ay eM Ee
But opposites do attract & I thought I loved that
Who knows, in due time we can get that thing back

…*Loveless*

Time does ease the pain
Although feelings do remain
Of course somethings change
Yet some memories just don't fade
Tears still fall as I think of you, but no one's here to dry them
They come, stay for a while, then disappear
Kind of like you did;
Here today gone tomorrow
I can't help these tears I cry
They just keep falling
Thinking of my "could've been" & how it will "never be"
I never thought I'd need a backup plan
At least not with you
Some fool I was, but never no more
They say never say never but of this I'm sure
I've changed once again & love has shown me something new
When you enter a relationship
The other person WILL change you!
Sometimes for the better. No. Always for the better
For I've learned many things from these partnerships I've been in
And knowledge is power;
Power to make changes in me, a new & better self
And what's better than that? Simply nothing else
No touch, No kiss, No body, No one.
Nothing can substitute for true self-love
The love you have for you, the love you have to give, the way you
love to love
Selfless Love, True Love, A love you've never felt
… Loveless

Being All Alone

Being all alone isn't really all that bad
You find the time to realize things about yourself you never had
Like the things that make you happy & things that make you cry
Being all alone will even help you to find the reasons why
Finding out these reasons, to some, may come as a surprise
Though this self awareness is more valuable than you may realize
Learning little secrets to obtain the ultimate grand prize
Of loving & knowing yourself through your own beautiful eyes
To grow comfortable with things that you may often compromise
In order to appease those around you; people often in disguise
Lovers, friends, & confidants, even family too
Sometimes in this unsure life, it is all about you
Into the light, out of the dark, & into the arms of mother
But remember when you were in the womb
There was not another
Going through life you live & learn, often surrounded by some
But when it comes to self & tests there's really always just one
Even on a team of many, you all put forth effort & try
But at the top of success there's always one who sits most high
One is just a number but more often it can be
A place where which you ultimately find the true importance
of "Me"
Being all alone doesn't necessarily have to be lonely
It can be a place of growth & even quite comforting
We say alone but in reality, GOD is always there
In the deepest times of uncertainty
You can sense HIM in the air
Or reach HIM through prayer,
Or even see HIM in a distant stare
GOD is always with you when you cannot even bear
Being all alone will always change the way you see
Because Being all alone is where 'You' finally meets 'me'

Beginning of the End

It's the beginning of the end
When lovers can't remain friends
And the pieces of your heart you begin to mend
It's a fucked up situation really to be in
Even more fucked up is the consideration of stayin'
Just to endure more pain
Fresh tear stains
All memories boxed up ready to set a blaze
All friends gone away; mom too
The only person that could really get you through
Cancer sucks and people suck more
My heart;
you ripped it, you shredded, you tore
And silly me, what do I do?
I give you more
Things from my heart
Things you don't ask for
But I won't take them back
That's how you expect me to act
But the kind of love I have doesn't work like that
From stranger to friend to lover and then
Again to stranger
My heart, my mind, my life in danger
This familiar feeling I remember again
The fucked up feeling of the beginning of the end.

About the Author

A native of Houston, TX, Hassen Gabriel Alli is a self-proclaimed hope-full romantic who has dealt with the cycles of love from early childhood crushes into the intricate relationships in his young adult life. Writing was always a passion and an outlet for emotions as he began to navigate relationships early on. This soon evolved into a way to communicate on a deeper level and convey thoughts and ideas to those in, near, and around the relationships he encountered.